THE
KISSING

OF
KISSING

multiverse

Series Editor
CHRIS MARTIN

THE
KISSING
OF
KISSING

poems

**Hannah
Emerson**

MILKWEED EDITIONS

Published 2022 by Milkweed Editions
Printed in the United States of America
Cover design by Mary Austin Speaker
Cover art by Mary Austin Speaker

Library of Congress Cataloging-in-Publication Data

Names: Emerson, Hannah, author. | Martin, Chris, 1977 August 11- series editor. | Nisinzweig, Aviv, editor.
Title: The kissing of kissing : poems / Hannah Emerson ; series editor, Chris Martin ; book editor, Aviv Nisinzweig.
Description: First edition. | Minneapolis, Minnesota : Milkweed Editions, 2022. | Series: Multiverse ; 1 | Summary: "In this remarkable debut, which marks the beginning of Multiverse-a literary series written and curated by the neurodivergent Hannah Emerson's poems keep, dream, bring, please, grownd, sing, kiss, and listen"-- Provided by publisher.
Identifiers: LCCN 2021037277 (print) | LCCN 2021037278 (ebook) | ISBN 9781571315496 (trade paperback) | ISBN 9781571317766 (ebook)
Subjects: LCGFT: Poetry.
Classification: LCC PS3605.M468 K57 2022 (print) | LCC PS3605.M468 (ebook) | DDC 811/.6--dc23
LC record available at https://lccn.loc.gov/2021037277
LC ebook record available at https://lccn.loc.gov/2021037278

Milkweed Editions is committed to ecological stewardship. We strive to align our book production practices with this principle, and to reduce the impact of our operations in the environment. We are a member of the Green Press Initiative, a nonprofit coalition of publishers, manufacturers, and authors working to protect the world's endangered forests and conserve natural resources.

CONTENTS

THE
KISSING

OF
KISSING

MY NAME BEGINS AGAIN

No Hannah oh I want
to make my life like

my name. Looking looking
to the beginning of the pleasing

moment that I become
my name. My name

my name my name. Yes
I want to be my name.

BECOMING MUD

Please be with me great free animals. I want to be
with you great being of light. Please see me great

nobody nobody nobody hell animals trying to go
to helpful keepers of the knowledge try to go

to the place in the mud that is where I try to live
in peace great mud of this great kissing loving

earth lovely messy yucky in mud on my face if
kissing mother loving me is the great animal

that is named Hannah. Please greet me in
the mud it is great mess please go to oh

the bucket to get the water to try to make
more mud yes. Please try to get the mud

helpful to you if you become mud too.
Please get that great animals are all

autistic. Please love poets we are the first
autistics. Love this secret no one knows it.

KISSING TENDRIL MIND

Please get that you get
that freedom is yearning
to grow yes yes yes. Please
get that kissing mind needs us
to kiss knowledge yes yes. Please

get that knowledge is the light
of the heart yes yes. Please get
that you need to go to the great great
great beautiful mother of kissing heart yes
yes. Please get that the mother helps us go
to the beautiful heart that really everything flows

through yes yes. Please get that trying flow
goes through the veins in us yes yes. Please get
that kissing kissing kissing heart loves us through that
flow of blood yes yes. Please get that kissing mother greets
your flowering thoughts yes yes. Please get that these flowers
are free yes yes. Please get that you help me grow into kissing
flower of thought and life yes yes. Please get that everything

is kissing flowers going to live and die yes yes. Please
get that flowers began in kissing life first yes yes. Please
get that there was nothing then growth happens great flowers
got to live here yes yes. Please get they are nothing but flowers
yes yes. Please get that nothing us helping great great great beautiful
flowers is us yes yes. Please get that kissing flowers help us to become
them yes yes. Please get that you help the flowers grow yes yes. Please
get that the light is the great great great nothing flower and tendril yes yes.

PERIPHERAL

Yes I prefer the peripheral
because it limits the vision.

It does focus my attention.
Direct looking just is too

much killing of the moment.
Looking oblique littles

the moment into many
helpful moments.

Moment moment moment
moment keep in the moment.

JUST HAPPY THAT LOVELY CHILDREN ARE DANCING

Love love love the rolling hills
kissing jutting
that make my great great great rolling dance
that I make my life
helping me dance dance dance
just dancing my life into being yes yes yes

Love that the mother is
kissing the dancing
that kisses me today yes yes

Love the kissing of kissing
loving the air
that greets our dance
that kisses the movements
that makes the air move
with me yes yes yes

Love the mother kissing us just
happy that lovely
children are dancing in the air kissing
lovely nothing as we
move to the calling of the wind
yes yes yes

Love the kissing kissing
kissing lovely kissing
in the movement that we
try to go to on these
hills of debris yes yes

Love the dripping of the drops
that are our thoughts
trying to cry our very very very hell
away yes yes

Love the light that is
in the yearning that is
dripping from the sky
yes yes

Love the kissing rain that is
the keeper of the kissing
thoughts of the sky
that cries for us today yes yes

Love the clouds that kiss us
into the thoughts that are
trying to make this
interesting yes yes

Love the drops of rain
that just sit on the branch
waiting to be called
to dance dance dance yes yes yes

Love mother greeting yearning
to help us go
to the nothing dance
becoming the freedom that is
in the great great great drop
of the movement
helping us go to the dance
going there dripping with the drowning

of our freedom that wants to go
to the dance dance trying to become
the dripping dance dance nothing
more yes yes yes

KEEP

Love the light nice
let it in. Go into
the halo. It is hotter
there. Look beyond it
to find your place
in the womb. Keep

cooking. I am a cook
cooking with beef.
Try it. It makes me
strong. As strong as
the cow. The smells
are the essence. Let's

go to the bedroom.
Look very hard to find
the place between
the pillow and hell.
Peaceful dreams live
in the great space

inside. Inside the place
where your insides come
out. Hard to do most
of the time. But so very
necessary. Close
the door. Let me be

please. It is a place
my place don't keep
bothering me because

it must be mine. I am
me here. Keep
out. Find your own

light.

HOW THE WORLD BEGAN

Please try to cut
yourself open
to find the blood
that is the color
of the molten rock
that is in all of us
yes – please try
to help the world
by heaving your
hatred on the flames
that burn in your town
yes yes – please try
to melt yes yes – please
try to grow into the stream
of molten life yes yes – please
try to help us make kissing
kissing volcano that loves
with way of floating hell
that we are now now
now yes yes yes –
please get that this
is how the world
began began
began yes yes –

A BLUE SOUND

Blue fish is swimming
jumping great keeping
the world from tilting

upside down. He greets
the dawn with the freedom
of life. He goes from life

to death. In one breath.
Please help me do
what you know. I am

blue too. I help the fish
live in the keeping
of the sound.

THE PATH OF PLEASE

Please get the freedom of nothing it is
great white snow on the world trying
to melt our minds into nothing yes

please get it is really important to say
yes. I want to go to the flake of
snow that indescribable thing

that we need to know if we are to melt
into nothing. Please find the flake
that takes to you the storm is

not it. Please shovel the pile of snow
to find your path yes. Please know
the white is the nothing of the

great really great great helpful kissing
universe yes yes yes yes white.
Please go to the melting

of the flake there you will find nothing
yes. Please find the melter of all
things the sun. Please go

to the light of the sun yes yes yes. Please
try to evaporate into the great universe.
Please try to help me do it too.

Please try to go to your light it is trying
to love you yes yes yes. Please free
yourself to go to the lovely flake

in your great mind and try to go
to the point where you began
this storm.

I LIVE IN THE WOODS OF MY WORDS

I live in the branches
of the trees. I live in
the great keeping
freedom of the really
helpful down yearning
in the grown of the forest
floor. The words fall
from the sky like snow
on this day. They become
the floor of the forest.
The ground from which
all things grow into
the towards. It is great
great dream of life
try to dream. I live
in each letter that is
where you will find me.
They have been given
to us as keys to the great
breathing hope of life.
I always wanted to live
there but couldn't live
there until the poetry
gave me life of words.

PLEASE TRY TO GO TO THE ROAD

that goes to the beginning
where we took our first breath

thousands of years ago yes yes.
Please try to go to the breath
that is trying to become the life

that is your dream yes yes.
Please try to hear your freedom
going through the tops of the trees
yes yes. Please try to get that

kissing the freedom that is
in the air that comes to you
through the road of breath
that was breathed months years
years helpfully you get that

they breathed us to be here
today yes yes. Please try
to become the breath that gives
helpful thoughts that are floating

towards you yes yes. Please
try to remember yes yes yes.
Please try to go to the breath

that is your road to the universe
that is in you yes yes. Please try

to imagine how big you are yes yes.

GIVENESS

denotes the great kissing
of great humans to get
unusually going to the heart
of the giving to the person
who needs to be forgiven.

Try to forgive helpful thought
helpful gesture to give to the person
who needs forgiveness. The king
keeps the jester there to remind
him of the helpful freedom of being

great fool. The queen is always
watching these two fools. O yes
great giving mother earth trying
to forgive the fools. The poets
here to keep telling the truth

of the keeping the life going
to survive. Poets give grounding
in helpful knowing the voice
of the universe. Please listen
to the poet because only way

to freedom from the fools. Just
keep the fools inside us loving
fool forgive him. It is ok to be
the fool you are helping
this great universe explode.

THE UNDERWORLD

Let's try to go
to the underworld
that melts us
into one yes
yes – love the mystery
that is there yes
yes – love the network
that is trying to connect
us yes yes – love
the most pleasing
network that grows
there yes yes – please
try to become the lovely
thoughts that are born
there yes yes – please
try to become the great
great great life that grows
from there yes yes – please
try to kiss the smelly
sweetness that is
there yes yes – please
please please grow
into the sweetness
that the universe wants
you to be be be be be
yes yes yes – please
try to understand that
you must grow down
to grow up yes yes

CONNEMARA PONY

It's beautiful how
the pony just lets me
look at how he peacefully

waits. Great horse
has deep feeling inside.

Tell me if you have poetry.
Tell me if you have more
to tell. Know that he is

beautiful. Is it a good life?
Is it peace? Peace like looking

into look of sea?
Is looking into looks
like living? I pour pours

into the sea, pours, pours,
presence is poetry.

TO GO TO

Please try to kiss the rhythm that makes the kissing

loving flow of the flooding blood intersect the making

of the flow of great making of the energy that flows

into my body giving me life that I need to be the poet

that I came here to be so I can yes yes. Please help

me help you by becoming the flow that is making us

kiss this kissing loving life that is our nothing life that is

a gift yes yes. Please try to kiss the energy that is

the kissing of the energy of the nothing that is

the kissing jutting life into something that is

inverting you into the first beat of your heart

that began this yearning that you kissed

to become the rhythm that is your portal

to this life yes. Please try to get that this

is the ultimate kissing kissing kissing gift

that the universe gives you yes yes.

Please try to be heroic and not give it

away to unconscious mess yes yes.

Please try to understand that you need

to do this using your energy to go

to the light that you are yes. Please try

to go to the kissing that is trying to help

you kiss this indescribable kissing job

that you make your life today yes.

THE SUN

Really everywhere
down to killing nobody
because loving keeps giving.

From deep down to high up go inward
for light. Keep drowning keep
growing keep listening
to the sun.

ANOTHER FREE BLUE VORTEX

Love to float
in the blue
of your soul
yes yes – love
to swim in
your thinking yes
yes – please try
to give me
permission to go
to the swimming
with you yes
yes – please try
to help me
get your great
great freedom
that you try
to swim in yes
yes – please try
to help me swim
the way you go
to the cause
that you need
to find in your
great great great
thought yes yes –
please try to go
to the vortex
that is trying
to take us
to another free
place where we

can become
one yes yes –
please try to let
go to help
yourself keep
from going down
the drain yes yes –

THE BEAUTIFUL BEAUTIFUL BEAUTIFUL
DREAMING BEAST

Please try to understand
that mother is kissing us
because making us
very nothing makes us
become the bridge
between the worlds
that are hard to be
sitting in but that is
autism that is the great
great great making
of the ground that is
making us become
the kissing that is
becoming the everything
that is trying to become
the opening of the freedom
that is the new window
to the beautiful kissing
that is the becoming
of the needed thinking
that is necessary
to make the bridge
into helpful grounding
that is the freedom of trying
to go to the kissing that is
needed to make us try
to become the beautiful
beautiful beautiful dreaming
beast that we are yes yes.

THROUGHT

Let's go to the place that is
loving you in a way that is
making you great new light
yes yes yes – let us help

ourselves hearing kissing
the great great great song
that is becoming the music
that is being born in this

world that you live in yes
yes yes – let's try to help
ourselves note the notes
that are being born in

you yes yes – love to listen
to the song that is loving
you into the song that you
must hear yes yes yes –

please try to play your music
really trying to become the music
that is trying to come to you
interiors going to the beautiful

beautiful beautiful mouth that lets
the sounds out into the universe
yes yes – please try to love the music
that is the new song that you need

to go to as your nothing freedom
song yes yes – love to hear you
making the sound that is making
the song that you want to try

to let go up your throught
at the becoming that is kissing
our thoughts that is the really
really helpful notes that needs

to be set free if you are going
to become the kissing song that
you need to sing to help yourself
make the song that you need

to sing to become the nothing
thoughts that is the happiness
that you want to feel in your very
very very beautiful beautiful mouth

that is the opening that loves
the world yes yes – please try
to sing sing sing your thoughts
that you need to let out yes yes

LANGUAGE OF LEAVES

Plants feel in graceful
poetry that they are life.
How each life has its own
reality. Some sounds
use words. I hear
the language of leaves.
It is deep and order
soft and real. Trees
yearn for peaceful
breeze. I open
our poetry.
Its life is
early. Its life
listens. Reality
soon ours. We
do our job.

TO BURROW

Please get that worms deep
down help the very great life
that we think only beauty
greets us on the lovely great
helpful helpful freedom of the dirt.
Lovely helpful dirt is the great
mother of great humans really
great helpful mother is full
of worms great mother is
beautiful full of great beautiful
pleasing great beautiful nothing
holes of great kissing worms
that bring life to us lovely
humans helping you get that
great great great lovely dirt
is great for you to get buried
in it if you dare to be with
the worms and mother yes.
Lovely great dirt is the great
great everything yes yes.
Please get that the worms
deep great beings giving
the inner helpful helpful new
channels for the new way
of life to be born into this
great great planet of ours
yes. Poetry is the worms
in our souls trying to burrow
new helpful lungs in our minds
great normals need this to breathe
to go forward into the future yes yes.

Please get that great great great mother
helps us to be brave to get great new nothing
life yes yes. Please get that the worms greet us
great great great great us yes. Please get that
you too can be become a worm too yes yes.

BETWEEN

Love the noun her trying
to be the noun that is
me keep trying but I feel
more like an it. Please
really feel like me is it.

Love being me beautiful
life makes me feel like
an it. Please stop seeing
me keep noticing being
the great moments I am

not an it. It great great
it it it it. It flows between
non-human animal tree
look to all the it it around
me they are great beings

that have been labeled
it too. Lovely tree lovely
rock lovely stream lovely
animal great mountain
we are all it because you

great spirit of great life
forget how to really are.
Please stop thinking
of yourself as an it.
It it beautiful it.

CENTER OF THE UNIVERSE

Please try to go
to hell frequently
because you will
find the light there

yes yes – please
try to kiss the ideas
that you find there
yes yes – please

try to get that
it is the center
of the universe
yes yes – please

try to help yourself
by kissing the hot hot
hot life that is born
there yes yes – please

try to yell in hell
yes yes – please
try to free yourself
by pouring yourself

into the gutter all
guttural guttural yell
yell yes yes – please
try to get that you

become the being
that you came there
to be yes yes – please
try to go to the great

great great fire that you
created because you
become the light
that the fire makes

inside of you
yes yes – please
try to kiss yourself
for going there

yes yes – please
get that you are
reborn there
yes yes – please

begin your day

THE OTHER WORLD

Lovely moth you kissed me then
kissed the other world in kissing
me to keep you loving me helping
me go to the place where you are

now yes yes – love that you loved
me me me yes yes – loving me
is the loving portal into the other
world kissing the poets who make

their music there yes yes – love
that you help me kiss the moths
that kiss the light yes yes – love
that you kiss the loving loving

loving that is making us nothing
nothing nothing yes yes – please
try to kiss yourself kissing your light
that gives poets the light to go

to the place to dive into the nothing
nothing moth yes yes – please try
to help me go to the place that you
now become yes yes – please try

to help me become you yes yes

LOVE IS

Love the flapping
orange into path
to the nothing yes
of kissing the warp
that is just waiting
yes – love the orange
yes yes – love the
yellow that our light
that is pouring from
life yes yes – love
in the wind yes

ORANGE

the dreaming the
path that we walk on
yes – love the making
and weft of the fabric
for us to unravel yes
dripping from our bodies
red of our blood and the
becoming one of the orange
our great great great helpful
love love is just flapping
yes –

IRISES

I deeply yearn to go
to new plane of being.
I go inside to find it.

O it looks like the only
place on earth. It looks
like nothing. It feels

like going I don't know
where. I want to find out.
Only the interesting deep

sounds.

FILL YOUR ARMS

Please try only to go
to the place that is just
trying kissing us yearning
to love this moment instead

of hating it yes. Please try to kiss
this place that is probing our sweet
soul that is trying to understand just
what the hell is going on yes. Please

help kiss the process that is happening
in this world now yes. Please fill your arms
with the bear the heart the monkey the horse
the kissing kissing kissing that they bring to us

today yes. Please try to help them get up to dance
in ward to find the strength that will find great great
great new wiring that is trying to become the nothing
air that we breathe that is sweat we need to let out yes.

Please try to go to the sweat helping yourself go to the salt
that will melt you yes. Please try to become the ocean that is
becoming yes yes that is becoming lovely life yes yes. Please
fill your arms trying to take in the nothing of everything yes yes.

BRING THE SPRING

Love to love
    the flight that
        is going to
            the feeder outside
                my window that
                    makes the freedom
going to the reality
    that is the reality
        that reason frees
            the song that
                is trying to
                    bring the spring
                        to us yes yes
Yearning to understand
    the flight that you take
        trying to go cutting
            the flight into
                the dreaming
                    that spring makes
its self the flight
    that is helping
        the freeing of
            the spring that
                goes to the sun
                  to ask for help
to drip the snow
    into the making
        of the pond that
            frees the spring
                to become the very
                    very very grounding

that is happening
            outside my window
                        just trying to kiss
                                    the green yes yes

                                    Please try to help
                                                the sun yearning

for the light
            of spring helps
                        the sun kiss
                                    us yes yes

                                    Please try to help
the reality that is
            trying to spring
                        into the flight
                                    that is trying
                                                to go to the sun
                                                            to make itself
the lovely spring
            that is trying
                        to give birth
                                    to the now now
                                                now to the making
that is the trying
            to keep the sun
                        freeing the birds
                                    to fly into the
                                                spring yes yes

Love the hard
        working chickadee
            really trying to make
                spring free everything
                    by itself yearning
for the freezing
        night to go to
            the pond and
                become the green
                    forming the egrets

that really want
        to fish there
            yes yes

                Please try to see
                    the freeing feathers
of the finches
        that are becoming
            the sun yes yes

                Please try
                    to understand
                        that the hawk
in the tree looking
        at the feathered
            little ones wants
                to fill their beaks
                    trying to bring
                        spring to her
nest too yes yes

Please try to make
the great great great
beautiful chirping
the grownding
that you free
yourself to take
flight into spring
yes yes

ANIMAL EAR

I hear great trying free sounds that you
do not hear yes it is

hard to try to live trying to hear the way
I do and you go listen

to me really hard to hear both at the same
time. I hear the vibrations

of your thoughts. I hear helpful plants
grow to the sun. I hear

the sun rays of healing light becoming
life freedom to breathe

life into hopeful hopeful life. I hear
the vibrations of fear

coming from everyone holding fear
in their mussy lives

of nothing life. I hear you trying to help
me great teachers

of the normal way of hearing. Please
learn from me because

it is hard being meet me great humans
just try greet me with fullness

of your lovely soul. When you turn
your thoughts to find reality of hearing

you will find me and your free animal
trying to hear helpful messages for you

from the animal trying to bite you.

POW POW POW POW

Please try to go to the beautiful kissing
helpful great great great nothing to find
the explosion
                    that you need

to do to explode
                              into the beautiful
you yes yes yes.

Please get that every act you
do is you
                    exploding into this

moment yes yes.

Please get that you help me explode
into myself of great poetry yes yes.

Please get kissing is exploding

                                        yes
                                        yes.
Please get that you need
to only explode
                        into yourself nothing
yes
        yes
                yes.

Please get that you need to go to the sun
to explode

                yes yes. Please get that

the sun is within yes yes yes.

Please get that you need to go to the sun
to let go yes

              yes

                  yes.

INTO THE TOWARDS

I go helped
by the keepers
of the beautiful

helpful beautiful helpful
thoughts of wonder.
The bird lands

on the top
of the tree
and realizes it

is me. It flies
into the window
and really gets

bumped into getting
its birdness. Then we
decide to become

one. Together we
become the dream
of this life

now. We melt
into the void
because that is

keeping reality real.

TEACH

Rain for opening left
inside easily sounds
leak. Prayer is leaking
water raises our learning
into the page. I listen
to ways of sound. I sound
each prayer to let all of
language answer me.
Teach our water its art.
Use questions.

HANNAH IS NEVER ONLY HANNAH

Please get that I am the trying
breeze going through the really
great great great world yes yes.

Please get that I am the drowning
helpful freedom of the storm yes
yes. Please get that I am the very

hot great great great sun yes yes.
Please get that I am the great
great great great ice that gives

you the freeze that you need
to get to melt into nothing yes
yes yes yes. Please get that I

am the sky great great great blue
nothing yes yes. Please get that
I am the grownd great great great

place helping you helping you
stand in grateful helpful helpful
helpful kissing her her her her

yes. Please get that you and I
greet the great great life from this
place of great great kissing life

life life life yes yes yes. Please
get that you are great form great
formless helping kissing kissing

great knowing the great great
great helpful kissing the trying
yes yes. Please get that helpful

loving thinking you help just help
kissing helpful loving great great
great world turn upside down yes

yes. Please get that you help me
by helping me turn upside down
too yes yes yes. Please get that

great great helpful kissing people
need to get that great helpful kissing
is turning kissing upside down yes

yes. Please get that helpful kissing
just needs to be gathered into this
helpful kissing trying hell of this life

to go forward to help me Hannah
Hannah Hannah yes yes. Please
get that you need loving kissing

to make you like me yes yes.
Please get that the kissing must
be great knotting of you me great

us together in this hell yes yes yes.
Please get that you kiss me helping
me kiss you yes yes.

THE EDGE

To be down
down look for
the grow

Help me look
help me go
to the edge.

Yes it is
lovely here
on the edge.

I want to go
to the edge
frequently.

It is keeping
the ground
growing now

more nothing.
How to take
nothing.

THE REASON YOU BECAME HUMAN

Kiss the feeling that is
                    here today helping us
go to the kissing beautiful
                    beautiful very trying place
of the party that you want
                    to go to on this labor day
        yes yes

Please try to become the breeze
                        that kisses you great great
great maker of the things we use
                        in our crowded lives of stuff
that is crowding our life stopping
                        us from being the lightness
in the air that helps you dance
                    yes yes

Please try to go to the party
                    naked do not feel ashamed
because we are our best
                    when we dream of a naked
kissing life without the stuff
                    that we become the stuff that
stops us from trying to dance
                    yes yes

Please try to understand that you
                        became human so you could
        dance dance dance
                    yes yes

COME HOME

Love that mother is becoming
the nothing that is trying to become
the great great great beautiful mother
that is freeing us to get
that freedom is the wild ready
trying to become the freedom
that is the kissing
freedom that we want
really trying to find the place
that is free from trying
to get that we become the dreaming
that is the really nothing
that is the freedom
that is becoming the freedom
that is trying to become the way
of our waking dream instead
of just in the dreams of the sleeping
tribes that are growing in that place
when we try to put your head on
the pillow and dream the wild
great great great freedom
that is the great great great becoming
the sun that is trying to give us
the light to see that we
help ourselves
helping the great great great
becoming burst becoming
the waking dream
that is the nothing
when we open our eyes
to try growing into the world

that is making the new freedom
that goes to the watering
that goes to the mother
that makes us cry
that make us try
to come home yes yes

LOVELY BURST

Please free me free air to be
like you helpful kissing verse.

Lovely great kissing burst of
helpful helpful great lovely

nothing just nothing great air.
Please talk to me great storm

blowing through lovely nothing
house of mine. Please try not

to go too fast great kissing
storm you get me to go out

to get blown by you. Please
great air become the ocean

that my song swims through
to find kissing ears to hear

me beautiful lovely thoughts
that want to fly into your yes.

SUGAR BEAT

Love how the hummingbird tries
to come into my painting

of the world that is
greeting us today yes yes

Love that the mother gives
mostly helpful goings of flight

that is going to take us
to the beautiful beautiful

beautiful center of the very
beautiful very pleasing jutting

home mother is going to take
us to the light of the buzzing

home that we need to go
to yes yes – look to the nothing

that is knotting the becomings
of your nothing life that you

very need to become
beautiful needing being

that you are yes yes – please
try to kiss yourself that is

in need of buzzing light
that you need to free

yourself to go to the sugar
water that is hanging outside

your window yes yes – please
try to kiss yourself sweet

hummingbird yes yes – please try
to go to the light that is

in you yes yes – please try
to make your heart beat

to the freedom of the flight
that is your life yes yes

CICADAS

Before you grow up shake
grow up and shout. Grow
up and free yourself to get

noticed. Please go to the tree
heave yourself. Place yourself
in the roots. You will come

out. Eventually.

OUR FEET BECOME THE MUSIC

Please try to hear
the notes that are
hovering in the breeze
yes yes – please try

to hear the kissing
loving helpful notes that
are going into our bodies
that are the becoming

of the language we
speak yes yes – please
try to hear the lightning
that is kissing us

through our bones yes
yes – love the language
that it spells in
the kissing mother

who is kissing us
through the mother
helping us get that
we are using our mother

to talk to our bones
that need the beautiful
mother to become
the word that I help

you with my words
that help us try
to get that this
is the connecting

to the place in where
we live yes yes –
please try to go
to your bones to

make the connection to
the mother that is
waiting for you there
yes yes – please try

to become the notes
that are making the earth
below our great great
mother notes that use

our feet to become
the music of our life
yes yes – please try
to go to the fly

that is noting the obvious
maker of the sounds
that just kiss our hearing
of the kissing maker

of the words that free
us to sing in this plane
of existence of the way
of our life yes yes –

please try to understand
that kissing the words
need to become one
with this mother earth

for us to note the nothing
life that great great great
helpful life is needing
to become the maker

of this life that we
become each moment
of our life yes yes –
please kiss the breeze

that loves you yes
yes – love that love
that is hugging us
on this plane of yearning

yes yes – please get
that kissing nature is
kissing us with their
song yes yes – please

get that the kissing
kissing great great mother
loves that we are
kissing her going to

this way of getting
of this idea yes
yes – please try to
keep the loving fly

close to you because
it brings the buzz
that sends the message
through our bones to

our beautiful
mind reminding
us who we are
yes yes

MUSIBILITY

is heavy freedom
going to the center
of the universe.

I really, I try
to understand, please
help me understand.

I want to go to the music.
The answer is there.
It is vibrating life.

KEEP YOURSELF AT THE BEGINNING OF THE BEGINNING

Please try to help me go to the joy that is trying
to go to the beautiful helpful helpful beginning
of the beginning of the very trying freedom
that we make our great great great light
that is nothing but the laughter that is
fooling us into believing that we go
to the trash bin that is your life
that become the treasures
that live in the bottom
of the bin that is
your life yes
yes yes
yes –
please
try to dive
down to the
beautiful muck
that helps you get
that the world was made
from the garbage at the bottom
of the universe that was boiling over
with joy that wanted to become you you
you yes yes yes – please try to go to the colors
that kiss you great great great person of the light
that is becoming you you you yes yes – please
try to keep yourself in the bottom of the bin
yes yes – please try to go to the kissing
muck that is very true to your life yes
yes – please try to meet me there
yes yes – please try to bring
your beautiful nothing
there yes yes

SACRED GROVE

Love that it is helping us go
        to the mother who is the freedom
that is dreaming the way back
        to the beast that is us yes yes yes

Love the dream that is in our gut
        that kisses us is going to kiss us
by trying to process this nothing
        helpful life in the way we read

the signs that are trying to become
        the ground that we note trying to help
the beautiful making of the tree that grows
        in us try to make helpful life become

        our being that is us yes yes

Love the making of the new
        ground that is the becoming
of the beast that is dreaming
        helping us go to the freedom

that it helps us go to that has
        always been there if you get
the new becoming the beautiful
        nothing that is the forest

that you really are yes yes

Make the mother try to go
        to the mother that tries to get you
to understand that you grow
        into the freedom that loves you

helping you get that nothing is
        the way you think it is yes yes

Love the nothing that is
        the union of the nothing
and the form that happens
        to appear as us yes yes

THE LISTENING WORLD

Say prayer for little
things, things that live
in deep hurt. Feelings
language take to lair.

Let it signal nothing's
light, I say for want
of light feelings. Is my
ear deep or deeper?

ACKNOWLEDGMENTS

Love the people that made this yearning book possible. Kiss you all yes yes.

Love my teachers from the past present and future yes yes.

Mother Earth makes me nothing yes yes.

Nate Trainor makes me great.

Aviv Nisinzweig makes love possible.

Chris Martin makes kissing easy.

Zan Emerson and Josh Intrator kiss me love me help me become me.

Dad makes me try harder.

Mom, great helpful kissing kissing great being that gives me life.

Zan Emerson

HANNAH EMERSON is a non-speaking autistic poet from Lafayette, New York. Her work has appeared in *BOMB Magazine*, Poetry Society of America, Literary Hub, *Brooklyn Rail*, and her own newsletter *The Kissing Nothing We Become*. Her chapbook, *You Are Helping This Great Universe Explode*, was published by Unrestricted Editions in 2020.

⅋ multiverse

Multiverse is a literary series devoted to different ways of languaging. It primarily emerges from the practices and creativity of neurodivergent, autistic, neuroqueer, mad, nonspeaking, and disabled cultures. The desire of Multiverse is to serially surface multiple universes of underheard language that might intersect, resonate, and aggregate toward liberatory futures. In other words, each book in the Multiverse series gestures toward a correspondence—human and more-than-human—that lovingly exceeds what is normal and normative in our society, questioning and augmenting what literary culture is, has been, and can be.

Founded as a nonprofit organization in 1980, Milkweed Editions is an independent publisher. Our mission is to identify, nurture and publish transformative literature, and build an engaged community around it.

Milkweed Editions is based in Bdé Óta Othúŋwe (Minneapolis) within Mní Sota Makhočhe, the traditional homeland of the Dakhóta people. Residing here since time immemorial, Dakhóta people still call Mní Sota Makhočhe home, with four federally recognized Dakhóta nations and many more Dakhóta people residing in what is now the state of Minnesota. Due to continued legacies of colonization, genocide, and forced removal, generations of Dakhóta people remain disenfranchised from their traditional homeland. Presently, Mní Sota Makhočhe has become a refuge and home for many Indigenous nations and peoples, including seven federally recognized Ojibwe nations. We humbly encourage our readers to reflect upon the historical legacies held in the lands they occupy.

milkweed.org

Milkweed Editions, an independent nonprofit publisher, gratefully acknowledges sustaining support from our Board of Directors; the Alan B. Slifka Foundation and its president, Riva Ariella Ritvo-Slifka; the Amazon Literary Partnership; the Ballard Spahr Foundation; *Copper Nickel*; the McKnight Foundation; the National Endowment for the Arts; the National Poetry Series; the Target Foundation; and other generous contributions from foundations, corporations, and individuals. Also, this activity is made possible by the voters of Minnesota through a Minnesota State Arts Board Operating Support grant, thanks to a legislative appropriation from the arts and cultural heritage fund. For a full listing of Milkweed Editions supporters, please visit milkweed.org.

Interior design by Tijqua Daiker and Mary Austin Speaker
Typeset in Jenson

Adobe Jenson was designed by Robert Slimbach for Adobe
and released in 1996. Slimbach based Jenson's roman styles
on a text face cut by fifteenth-century type designer Nicolas Jenson,
and its italics are based on type created by Ludovico Vicentino
degli Arrighi, a late fifteenth-century papal scribe
and type designer.

Printed in the USA
CPSIA information can be obtained
at www.ICGtesting.com
JSHW021629240324
59808JS00003B/5